★★★ ABRAMS TANKS

BY JACK DAVID

BELLWETHER MEDIA · MINNEAPOLIS, MN

E
[R/2]

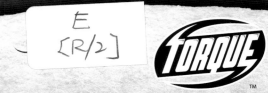
TM

Are you ready to take it to the extreme?
Torque books thrust you into the action-packed
world of sports, vehicles, and adventure. These books
may include dirt, smoke, fire, and dangerous stunts.
WARNING: read at your own risk.

Library of Congress Cataloging-in-Publication Data

David, Jack, 1968-
  Abrams tanks / by Jack David.
    p. cm. -- (Torque, military machines)
  Summary: "Explains the technologies and capabilities of the latest generation of military ve-
hicles. Intended for grades 3 through 7 "--Provided by publisher.
  Includes bibliographical references and index.
  ISBN-13: 978-1-60014-101-0 (hbk. : alk. paper)
  ISBN-10: 1-60014-101-3 (hbk. : alk. paper)
1. M1 (Tank)--Juvenile literature. 2. Tanks (Military science)--Juvenile literature. I. Title.
  UG446.5.D328 2008
  623.7'4752--dc22
                                                                        2007012012

This edition first published in 2008 by Bellwether Media.

The photographs in this book are reproduced through the courtesy of the United States Department of
Defense.

CONTENTS

THE ABRAMS IN ACTION 4

MAIN BATTLE TANK 8

WEAPONS....................12

ABRAMS MISSIONS 18

GLOSSARY 22

TO LEARN MORE 23

INDEX 24

THE ABRAMS IN ACTION

A long line of U.S. M1 Abrams tanks heads into battle. They roll steadily toward the desert battleground. A line of T-72 tanks stands waiting on the other side.

Abrams tanks are protected by a composite armor made of steel and ceramic.

The battleground is set. The Abrams tanks come to a stop. They begin to fire. The air is filled with the booming of their **main guns**. Huge shells smash into the T-72 tanks with amazing accuracy. The T-72s are no match for the Abrams tanks. Within minutes all of the T-72s are destroyed. Not one Abrams tank is damaged.

MAIN BATTLE TANK

Tanks are the biggest ground vehicle in any army. They are also the most powerful. They play a huge role in ground battles. No tank is more feared than the U.S. Army's M1 Abrams. It has tough **armor**, several weapons, and a powerful engine. These features make it the world's strongest tank.

An Abrams tank costs up to $4.2 million per tank.

There are four soldiers in an M1 Abrams crew. The commander is in charge of the tank. The driver steers it. The loader and gunner work together to load and fire the weapons. The crew members must work together to accomplish their **mission** and keep the crew safe.

WEAPONS

A tank's main gun is its most important weapon. The main gun sits on a **turret** on top of the tank. The gunner aims and fires the main gun from inside the tank. The gun shoots 120-millimeter shells. These huge bullets can hit targets more than two miles (3.2 kilometers) away.

The Abrams tank protects the crew from biological, chemical, and nuclear weapons.

A soldier loads the Abrams with weapons.

The loader loads the main gun.

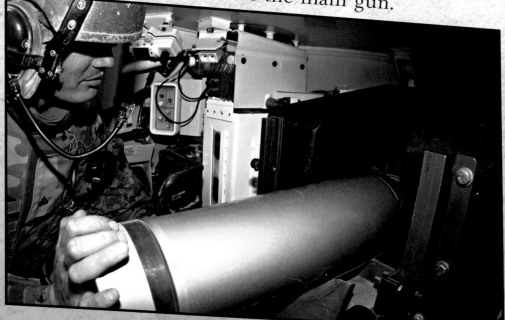

The Abrams also has a smoke **grenade** launcher. Smoke grenades cover an area in thick smoke. The Abrams tank can move through the smoke without being seen or targeted by enemy weapons.

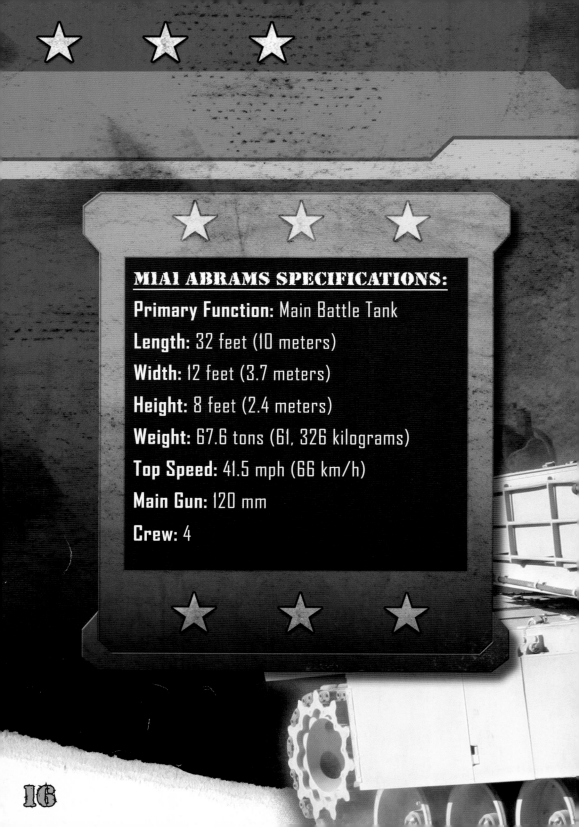

M1A1 ABRAMS SPECIFICATIONS:

Primary Function: Main Battle Tank

Length: 32 feet (10 meters)

Width: 12 feet (3.7 meters)

Height: 8 feet (2.4 meters)

Weight: 67.6 tons (61, 326 kilograms)

Top Speed: 41.5 mph (66 km/h)

Main Gun: 120 mm

Crew: 4

Two **machine guns** sit on top of the Abrams. They are used for fighting closer to the target. Strong armor and a powerful engine are also critical to the Abrams' success in battle.

ABRAMS MISSIONS

The Abrams has been in army service since 1981. It saw heavy action in the first Gulf War in 1991. It was almost unstoppable. Abrams tanks destroyed more than 100 Iraqi tanks in the Battle of Medina Ridge on February 27, 1991. Not a single Abrams was lost in the battle.

★ FAST FACT ★

The turret of an Abrams tank can rotate a full 360 degrees.

The Abrams is the U.S. Army's most important tank. It goes anywhere ground forces are needed. It can be used for attack or defense. Its firepower and strong armor make it a valuable military vehicle.

GLOSSARY

armor—protective plating

grenade—a smoky explosive that can be launched or thrown

machine gun—an automatic weapon that rapidly fires bullets

main gun—the large gun on top of a tank

mission—a military task

turret—the rotating part on top of a tank that holds the main gun

TO LEARN MORE

AT THE LIBRARY
Baker, David. *The M1A1 Abrams Tank*. Vero Beach, Fla.: Rourke, 2007

Braulick, Carrie A. *U.S. Army Tanks*. Mankato, Minn.: Blazers, 2006.

Budd. E.S. *Tanks*. Chanhassen, Minn.: Child's World, 2002.

ON THE WEB
Learning more about military machines is as easy as 1, 2, 3.

1. Go to www.factsurfer.com

2. Enter "military machines" into search box.

3. Click the "Surf" button and you will see a list of related web sites.

With factsurfer.com, finding more information is just a click away.

INDEX

accuracy, 7
armor, 5, 8, 17, 21
army, 8, 18
battle, 4, 8, 17, 18
Battle of Medina Ridge, 18
biological weapons, 13
chemical weapons, 13
commander, 10
crew, 10, 13, 14, 16
defense, 21
desert, 4
driver, 10
enemy weapons, 15
engine, 8, 17
features, 8
firepower, 21
ground forces, 21
Gulf War, 18
gunner, 10, 12

Iraqi tanks, 18
main gun, 7, 12, 14
machine gun, 17
mission, 10
nuclear weapons, 13
shells, 7, 12
smoke grenade, 15
T-72 tanks, 4, 7
targets, 12, 17
turret, 12, 18
U.S. Army, 8, 21
weapons, 8, 10, 12, 13, 14, 15